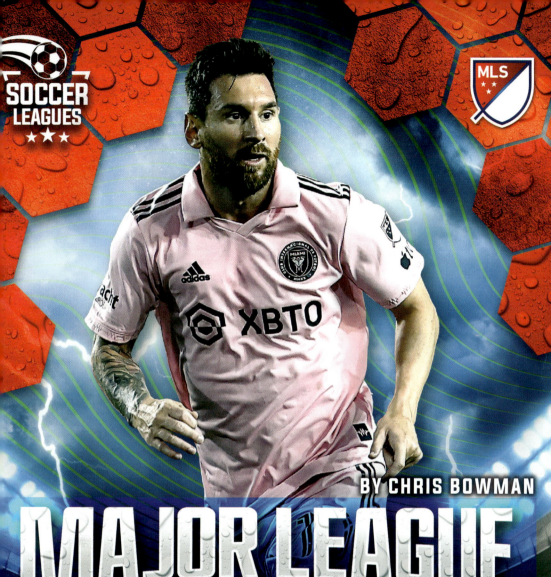

BY CHRIS BOWMAN

MAJOR LEAGUE SOCCER

BELLWETHER MEDIA • MINNEAPOLIS, MN

Torque brims with excitement perfect for thrill-seekers of all kinds. Discover daring survival skills, explore uncharted worlds, and marvel at mighty engines and extreme sports. In *Torque* books, anything can happen. Are you ready?

This edition first published in 2025 by Bellwether Media, Inc.

No part of this publication may be reproduced in whole or in part without written permission of the publisher. For information regarding permission, write to Bellwether Media, Inc., Attention: Permissions Department, 6012 Blue Circle Drive, Minnetonka, MN 55343.

Library of Congress Cataloging-in-Publication Data

Names: Bowman, Chris, author.
Title: Major league soccer / by Chris Bowman.
Description: Minneapolis, MN : Bellwether Media, Inc., 2025. | Series: Torque: Soccer leagues | Includes bibliographical references and index. | Audience: Ages 7-12 | Audience: Grades 4-6 | Summary: "Engaging images accompany information about Major League Soccer. The combination of high-interest subject matter and light text is intended for students in grades 3 through 7"– Provided by publisher.
Identifiers: LCCN 2024022493 (print) | LCCN 2024022494 (ebook) | ISBN 9798893040241 (library binding) | ISBN 9781644879603 (ebook)
Subjects: LCSH: Major League Soccer (Organization)–Juvenile literature. | Soccer–United States–History–Juvenile literature.
Classification: LCC GV943.55.M34 B69 2025 (print) | LCC GV943.55.M34 (ebook) | DDC 796.334/64–dc23/eng/20240524
LC record available at https://lccn.loc.gov/2024022493
LC ebook record available at https://lccn.loc.gov/2024022494

Text copyright © 2025 by Bellwether Media, Inc. TORQUE and associated logos are trademarks and/or registered trademarks of Bellwether Media, Inc. Bellwether Media is a division of Chrysalis Education Group.

Editor: Kieran Downs   Designer: Gabriel Hilger

Printed in the United States of America, North Mankato, MN.

TABLE OF CONTENTS

FOR THE WIN	4
WHAT IS MAJOR LEAGUE SOCCER?	6
HISTORY OF MAJOR LEAGUE SOCCER	8
MAJOR LEAGUE SOCCER TODAY	12
FAST FACTS	20
GLOSSARY	22
TO LEARN MORE	23
INDEX	24

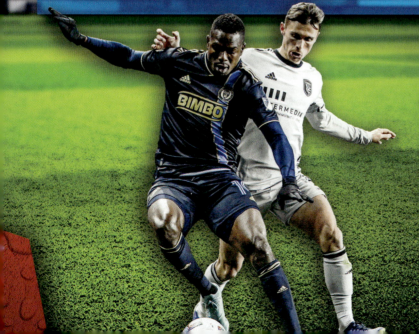

FOR THE WIN

It is the 2023 Major League Soccer (MLS) Cup. The Columbus Crew has been awarded a **penalty kick**. They take the kick. It goes in! The Crew leads LAFC.

The Crew scores another **goal** soon after. Then LAFC scores one of their own. It is a close match. But the Crew win their third MLS Cup!

WHAT IS MAJOR LEAGUE SOCCER?

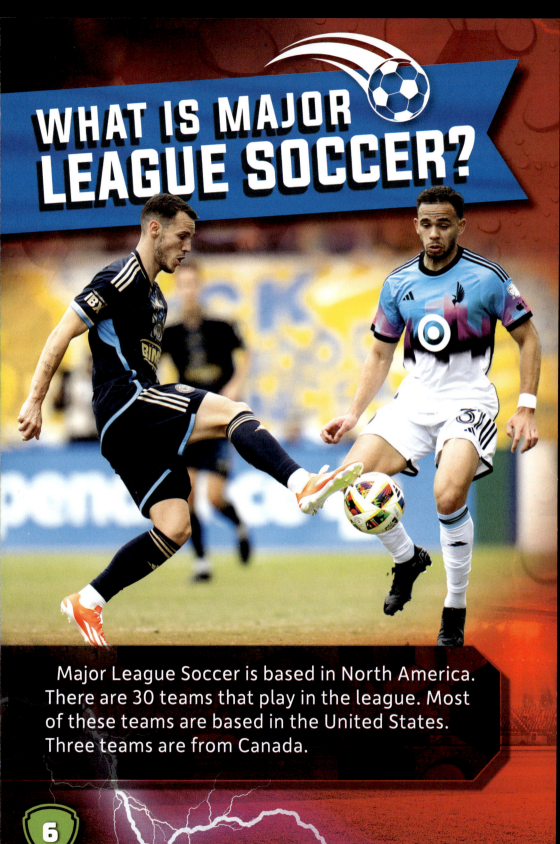

Major League Soccer is based in North America. There are 30 teams that play in the league. Most of these teams are based in the United States. Three teams are from Canada.

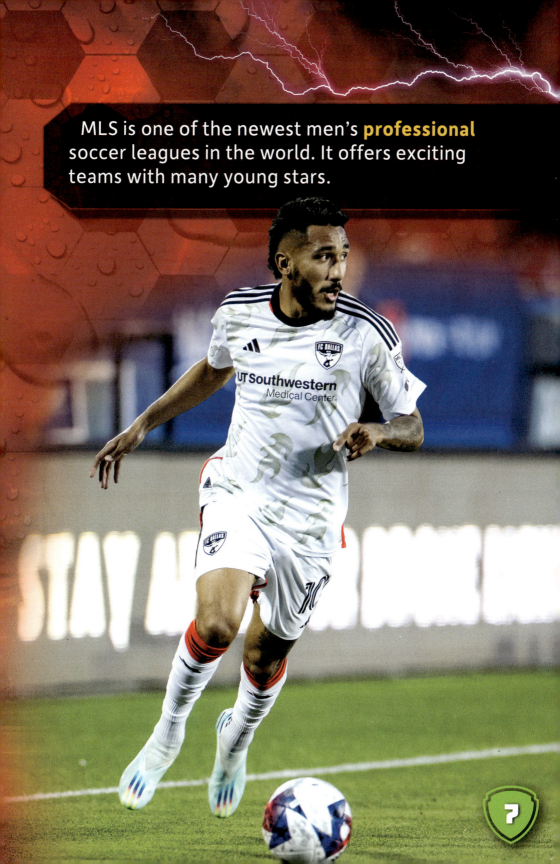

MLS is one of the newest men's **professional** soccer leagues in the world. It offers exciting teams with many young stars.

HISTORY OF MAJOR LEAGUE SOCCER

The idea for MLS began in the early 1990s. The U.S. wanted to host the 1994 **World Cup**. In exchange, the country agreed to form a **topflight** professional league.

The league's first matches were played in 1996. There were only 10 teams in its first year. Two more teams joined the league the following year.

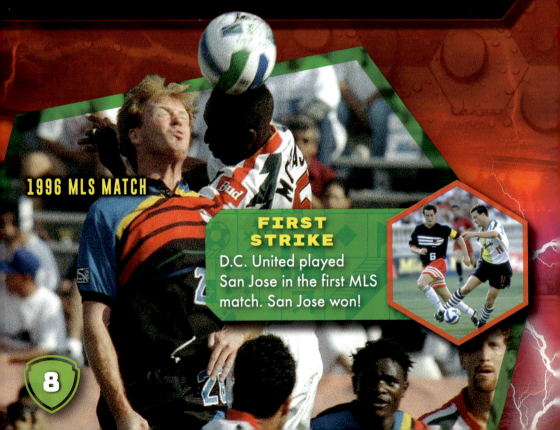

1996 MLS MATCH

FIRST STRIKE
D.C. United played San Jose in the first MLS match. San Jose won!

FOUNDING TEAMS

- COLORADO RAPIDS
- COLUMBUS CREW
- DALLAS BURN
- D.C. UNITED
- KANSAS CITY WIZARDS
- LOS ANGELES GALAXY
- NEW ENGLAND REVOLUTION
- NEW YORK/NEW JERSEY METROSTARS
- SAN JOSE CLASH
- TAMPA BAY MUTINY

The league struggled to gain new fans early on. Soccer was not popular in the U.S. MLS lost money for many years.

In 2007, MLS changed its rules to allow teams to pay more money to star players. This helped bring new star players to the league. The league continued to grow. In 2025, it reached 30 teams.

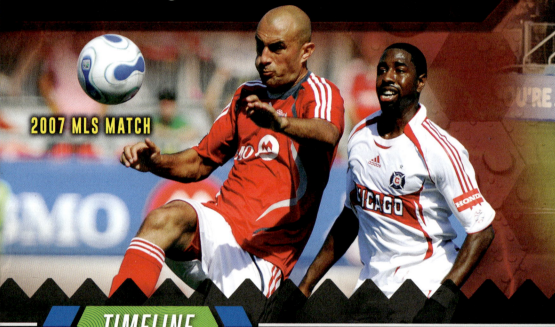

2007 MLS MATCH

TIMELINE

1994
The U.S. hosts the World Cup

1996
MLS begins its first season of play with 10 teams

1998
Two new teams join the league

10

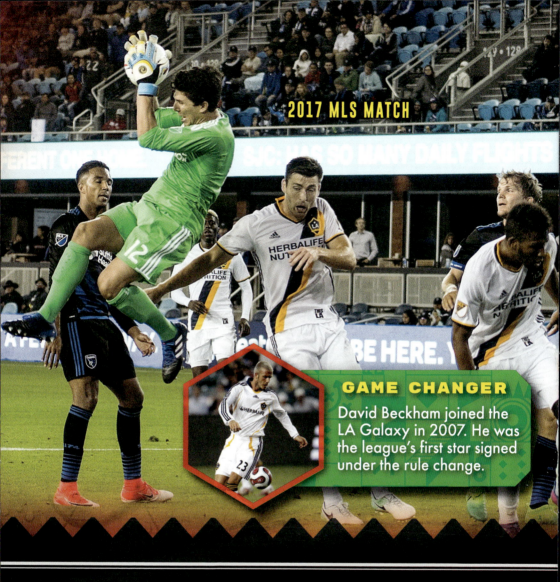

2017 MLS MATCH

GAME CHANGER

David Beckham joined the LA Galaxy in 2007. He was the league's first star signed under the rule change.

2007
A rule change allows teams to spend more on star players

2025
MLS adds its 30th team, San Diego FC

MAJOR LEAGUE SOCCER TODAY

There are 34 matches in an MLS season. The regular season begins in late February and ends in October. Teams play in one of two **conferences**.

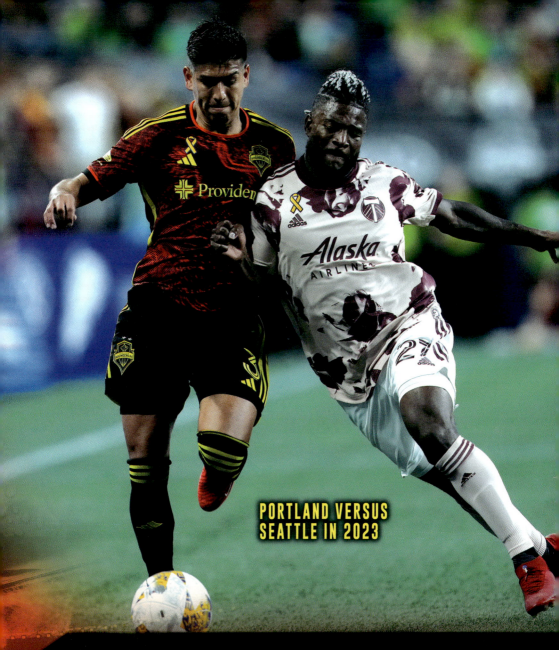

PORTLAND VERSUS SEATTLE IN 2023

MLS has a **rivalry** week in May. Most rivalries in MLS are based on where the teams are from. One of the biggest rivalries is between Seattle and Portland.

2022 ALL-STAR GAME

There is a break in MLS matches from late July to late August. The MLS **All-Star Game** is played early in this break.

The All-Star Game usually has the best players in MLS play against a team from a European league. Sometimes it is played against an All-Star team from another league.

2023 ALL-STAR GAME

NUMBERS GAME
Around 20,000 fans show up to most MLS matches.

The top seven teams in each conference qualify for Round 1 of the MLS Cup **Playoffs**. The eighth and ninth place teams play in the **Wild Card** matches. The winners reach Round 1.

Teams play a best-of-three **elimination** series in Round 1. They play one elimination game in the next two rounds. The winners of each conference play in the MLS Cup.

2023 MLS CUP PLAYOFFS

MLS CUP PLAYOFFS

1. TOP SEVEN
The top seven teams reach Round 1.

2. WILD CARD MATCHES
The eighth and ninth place teams play in the Wild Card matches with the winner going to Round 1.

3. MLS CUP
Teams play in three elimination rounds and the winners of each conference play in the MLS Cup.

MLS gives out other awards each season. The team with the most points at the end of the regular season wins the Supporters' Shield. The **Most Valuable Player** award goes to the year's best player.

Fans enjoy supporting their teams with songs and chants. Some fans even bring large flags. There are many ways to cheer on your favorite MLS players!

TOP PLAYERS

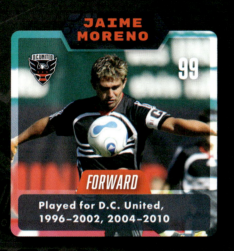

JAIME MORENO — 99
FORWARD
Played for D.C. United, 1996–2002, 2004–2010

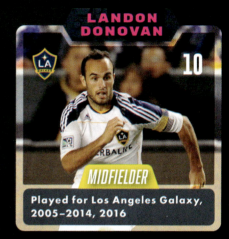

LANDON DONOVAN — 10
MIDFIELDER
Played for Los Angeles Galaxy, 2005–2014, 2016

CHRIS WONDOLOWSKI — 8
FORWARD
Played for San Jose Earthquakes, 2005, 2009–2021

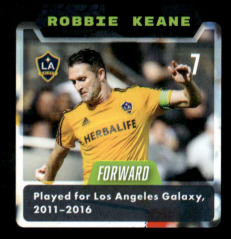

ROBBIE KEANE — 7
FORWARD
Played for Los Angeles Galaxy, 2011–2016

DIEGO VALERI — 8
MIDFIELDER
Played for Portland Timbers, 2013–2021

19

FAST FACTS

NUMBER OF TEAMS	30
YEAR STARTED	1996

LARGEST STADIUM

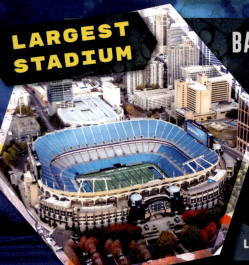

★ ★ ★
BANK OF AMERICA STADIUM
CHARLOTTE FC

Capacity: about 75,000 people
Location: Charlotte, North Carolina

CLUB RECORDS
(AS OF 2023)

CLUBS WITH MOST APPEARANCES — 29
COLORADO RAPIDS, COLUMBUS CREW, D.C. UNITED, FC DALLAS, SPORTING KANSAS CITY, LA GALAXY, NEW ENGLAND REVOLUTION, NEW YORK RED BULLS

CLUB WITH MOST CHAMPIONSHIPS — 5
LA GALAXY

FIRST CHAMPION
D.C. UNITED

CLUBS THAT HAVE PARTICIPATED IN THE LEAGUE — 33

INDIVIDUAL RECORDS
(AS OF 2023)

Most career league goals
Chris Wondolowski: 171 goals

Most goals scored in a single season
Carlos Vela: 34 goals

Fastest goal scored
Mike Grella: 7 seconds

Person with most league appearances
Nick Rimando: 514 Appearances

GLOSSARY

All-Star Game—a game between the best players in a league

conferences—groups of sports teams that play each other often

elimination—related to a type of match where the loser exits the series

goal—a score in soccer; a player scores a goal by sending the ball into the other team's net.

most valuable player—the best player in a year, game, or series; the most valuable player is often called the MVP.

penalty kick—a free kick awarded after a foul by an opponent within the penalty area

playoffs—matches played after the regular season is over; playoff matches determine which team plays in the championship match.

professional—related to a player or team that makes money playing a sport

rivalry—a long-standing competition between teams

topflight—related to the highest level of play

Wild Card—related to matches played to decide which teams get the last spots in the playoffs

World Cup—an international soccer competition held every four years; the World Cup is the world's largest soccer tournament.

TO LEARN MORE

AT THE LIBRARY

Adamson, Thomas K. *Lionel Messi*. Minneapolis, Minn.: Bellwether Media, 2023.

Gish, Ashley. *National Women's Soccer League*. Minneapolis, Minn.: Bellwether Media, 2025.

Golkar, Golriz. *Alex Morgan*. Minneapolis, Minn.: Bellwether Media, 2024.

ON THE WEB

FACTSURFER

Factsurfer.com gives you a safe, fun way to find more information.

1. Go to www.factsurfer.com

2. Enter "Major League Soccer" into the search box and click 🔍.

3. Select your book cover to see a list of related content.

INDEX

All-Star Game, 14, 15

Beckham, David, 11

Canada, 6

conferences, 12, 16

fans, 10, 15, 18

fast facts, 20–21

founding teams, 9

goal, 4

history, 4, 8, 9, 10, 11

match, 4, 8, 11, 12, 14, 15, 16

MLS Cup, 4, 16, 17

money, 10

Most Valuable Player, 18

North America, 6

penalty kick, 4

players, 7, 10, 11, 15, 18, 19

playoffs, 16, 17

rivalry week, 13

rules, 10, 11

season, 12

Supporters' Shield, 18

teams, 4, 6, 7, 8, 9, 10, 11, 12, 13, 15, 16, 18

timeline, 10–11

top players, 19

United States, 6, 8, 10

Wild Card matches, 16

World Cup, 8

The images in this book are reproduced through the courtesy of: Rich Graessle/ Icon Sportswire/ AP Images, cover; Don Mennig/ Alamy, pp. 3, 12; Sue Ogrocki/ AP Images, p. 4; Kindell Buchanan/ Alamy, pp. 4-5; Kyle Rodden/ AP Images, p. 6; Matthew Visinsky/ Icon Sportswire/ AP Images, p. 7; Chris Martinez/ AP Images, p. 8 (1996 MLS match); George Tiedemann/ Contributor/ Getty, p. 8 (First Strike); Major League Soccer/ Wiki Commons, pp. 9 (MLS team logos), 11 (2025); Aaron Harris/ AP Images, p. 10 (2007 MLS match); Lois Bernstein/ AP Images, p. 10 (1994); KEVORK DJANSEZIAN/ AP Images, pp. 10 (1996), 11 (Game Changer); PA Images/ Alamy, p. 10 (1998); Rob Sirota/ AP Images, p. 11 (2017 MLS match); Francis Specker/ Alamy, p. 11 (2007); Jeff Halstead/ Icon Sportswire/ AP Images, p. 13; Bailey Hillesheim/ AP Images, p. 14; Jose L. Argueta/ ISI Photos/ Contributor/ Getty, p. 15 (2023 All-Star Game); Cal Sport Media/ Alamy, pp. 15 (Numbers Game), 19 (Chris Wondolowski, Robbie Keane, Diego Valeri), 21 (Chris Wondolowski, Carlos Vela, Nick Rimando); Michael Wyke/ AP Images, p. 16; Alex Kormann/ AP Images, p. 18; tony quinn/ Alamy, p. 19 (Jamie Moreno); Abaca Press/ Alamy, p. 19 (Landon Donovan); Ben Nichols/ Alamy, p. 20; Grindstone Media Group, p. 20 (Bank of America Stadium); Brent Clark/ Alamy, p. 21 (Mike Grella); Xinhua/ Alamy, p. 23.